KIDS CAN COPE

Face Your Fears

by Gill Hasson

illustrated by Sarah Jennings

Franklin Watts
First published in Great Britain in 2020
by The Watts Publishing Group

Series Editor: Jackie Hamley
Series Designer: Cathryn Gilbert

A CIP catalogue record for this book is
available from the British Library.

ISBN 978 1 4451 6609 4 (hbk)
ISBN 978 1 4451 6610 0 (pbk)

Printed in China

Franklin Watts
An imprint of
Hachette Children's Group
Part of The Watts Publishing Group
Carmelite House
50 Victoria Embankment
London EC4Y 0DZ

An Hachette UK Company
www.hachette.co.uk

www.franklinwatts.co.uk

Face Your Fears

by Gill Hasson

illustrated by Sarah Jennings

Do you ever feel scared? Did you know that everybody feels afraid sometimes?

This book can help you feel less frightened and really face your fears.

Do you get scared?

Being scared or afraid is a feeling that everyone has. We all get scared when we think something might hurt us or harm us. We feel afraid and we want to stay safe!

Sometimes the things that we're scared of are real. Things like spiders and dogs, thunder and lightning.

Sometimes we get scared about things that are not real, like monsters. They're not real, but we feel scared of them anyway.

Other times we feel afraid of things that might happen but probably won't, like a volcano erupting.

How do you feel when you're scared?

When you're scared, it doesn't feel nice! Your heart might start thumping and your tummy might feel like it's in knots. You may feel hot or cold and get goosebumps, and feel the hair on your body standing on end.

You might feel embarrassed that you're scared because you think you should be tougher or stronger.

I might get hurt!

What do you do when you're scared?

Besides thinking scary thoughts and feeling funny, you might not want to go to places or do things.

Maybe you don't want to go to school because you have a new teacher and you don't know him or her very well.

Welcome, Everyone!

When you're afraid, it can even be hard to do things that could be fun. Perhaps you're scared of loud noises so you don't want to go to a firework display.

It's not silly to feel scared

Sometimes, if you tell people that you're scared,
they might say things like, "Stop being a baby!"
"Don't be scared!" "You're being silly!"

But when they say things like
that, it doesn't help.
It doesn't make the fear
go away.

The dentist won't hurt you.
You'll be okay!

Feeling scared is not silly. Remember, everyone feels scared sometimes. The most important thing is to do something about your fear so you can feel happy and safe.

Run around the spider.

Getting help with your fears

Even if you're worried that people will say there's nothing to be scared of, or that you're being silly, DO tell someone when you feel afraid.

Make sure you find someone you like and trust. This person could be a friend, teacher or someone in your family. If they haven't got time to talk about it right then, ask when a better time would be to talk.

Say, "I'm scared of something. Can I talk to you about it?"
Tell them what you're afraid of and what you think might
happen. Ask them to help you think what you could do
to be less afraid.

If you can't talk to someone you know and trust,
you can talk to someone on the phone or by email.
Look at the back of this book for information about this.

Take action to feel less afraid

Sometimes the worst thing about feeling scared is that you don't know what to do. But the good news is that you CAN do things to feel less afraid.

For some fears, you can take action to help yourself.

Billie is afraid of the dark. Together with her dad, Billie came up with some ideas to help her cope with her fears and get to sleep more easily.

They decided that Billie could keep the bedroom door open and have a nightlight at the side of her bed so that it wasn't too dark in the room.

My bedtime plan

Billie's dad agreed that Billie could also read or listen to a story to help her stop thinking about scary things.

Set yourself a goal

Sometimes, the things you are scared of will not go away. But you can still think of ways to feel less frightened.

If you can, ask someone else – a grown-up or a friend – to help you deal with what you're scared of so that you can feel happier and safer.

Start by thinking and talking about what you'd like to be able to do without being scared. This is your goal. It might help you to write it down.

Maybe you want to play at your friend's house but you're afraid of his pet rat.

Maybe you want to be able to go on an escalator or rollercoaster without being afraid.

Think of some things you could do that might help you, such as counting silently in your head, breathing deeply or having someone with you to hold your hand.

Take steps towards feeling less scared

For some fears, you can try getting used to doing the thing that frightens you.

This means that you start with something that's only a little scary and then take small steps towards doing the thing that is the scariest for you right now.

You go from one step to the next until you can do the thing you're afraid of and hardly be scared at all.

Tom wanted to play his guitar
in the school concert.
But he was afraid to play in
front of people.

Over time, he played in front
of larger and larger groups.
First, he just played in front
of his mum, then his family,
then his class.

Next, he played in front
of the whole school.

Finally, he played in front
of the school and all
the parents!

Getting used to the thing you're
afraid of might take quite a lot of
time. You might need to repeat some
steps. Take as much time as you need.

Build up your courage

You can help yourself take each step by having courage. This means doing something even though you feel a bit scared.

Can you remember when you've been worried about doing something but you were brave and did it anyway? Maybe you were scared of water but you wanted to learn to swim. You were afraid but with each swimming lesson you felt less frightened and more confident.

To help you build up your courage, you can tell yourself things like, "I can do this", "It will be okay", "I'm going to be brave."

I can do this!

Taking a big breath just before you do something can help, too. Take a deep breath, hold it, and count to three. As you breathe out, do the thing that you're scared to do.

If you think you're too scared to even try something, see if you can try it just for a short amount of time. Even just 5 seconds. Once you can handle 5 seconds, try it for 10 seconds, then 20.

Also, think about how good you'll feel when you've done the thing that frightened you.

See how well you're doing!

Whenever you're brave and manage to do something you were a bit scared of, be sure to tell yourself how well you did. Tell yourself, "I was brave and I did well!"

You might like to make a 'Facing Fears' poster that can show each time you've been brave and taken a step towards your goal.

On your poster, write down what it is you'd like to be able to do. Then write down each step you plan to take. Each time you are brave and take a step, give yourself a star. Remember – take as much time as you need for each step, and repeat each step as many times as you want.

Goal: To feel OK in the water

- ⭐ Sit by the pool
- ⭐ Get into the pool
- ⭐ Put a toy into the pool
- ○ Put my head in the water
- ○ Jump into the water to a grown-up
- ○ Float on back with Dad holding me

Learn about your fear

Another thing you can do is to ask a grown-up to help you understand why some things are scary. Often, when you understand how and why something happens, it can be less frightening.

For example, if you were afraid of thunder and lightning, you could find out what makes the big loud sounds and the bright flashes that come with thunder and lightning. You could look in a book, or search on the Internet.

Sometimes, you might watch TV and hear about things like wars and attacks, or earthquakes and floods, and feel scared.
It's important to talk to a grown-up about these things.

Bad things do happen, but we are safe here right now.

Tell the adult you're worried and afraid. Ask how likely it is that these things will happen to you, or to your family and friends.

Stop scary thoughts

Sometimes you might be busy with something and suddenly start to worry about a scary thing happening. Maybe you are at school, or playing with your friends, when you have a frightening thought.

When scary thoughts suddenly pop into your mind like this, you can tell yourself, " Stop! I'm not going to let myself feel scared right now." Remind yourself that whatever it is you're scared of, you CAN do something about it. You might not be able to do something right then, but you can do something later.
(Page 30 has some reminders about what to do.)

Tell the scary thoughts "Go away! I'm not listening." Then go back to what you were doing.

Keep safe

Remember, it's normal to be scared. Being afraid is a feeling that everyone has. In fact, fear can protect us. It can warn us to keep ourselves safe from something that could hurt us.

It's important to know that there are times when it's right to be afraid and scared of doing something.

If you're afraid to cross over the middle of a busy road, that's good! Don't do it, not even if someone dares you. Find a safe place to cross instead.

And if you feel worried and scared because of something you've seen on screen, or if you feel scared and afraid of someone you know or someone on the computer, always tell a grown-up about it.

Face Your Fears

It might help you to know that other children and grown-ups have overcome their fears by using ideas like the ones in this book. You can, too. Here's a reminder:

- Talk to someone you trust about how you feel.

- Take action to help you be less scared and afraid of something. Make a plan on your own or with someone else's help.

- Take steps towards doing something that scares you. Take one step at a time until you can do the thing you're afraid of and hardly be scared at all.

- Build up your courage. When you do something that you're still a bit scared of, take a big breath and tell yourself, "I can do this" and "It will be okay".

- Ask a grown-up to help you understand why some things are scary.

- When fears crop up in your mind, remind yourself that you can face them and find help to feel less afraid. Tell scary thoughts, "Go away! I'll deal with you later."

If your fears feel too big to handle, ask a grown-up for help. If you don't feel you can ask anyone you know, you can call ChildLine on 0800 1111, or go to www.childline.org.uk to sign up and send an email or post on the message boards. They will listen to you and give you some help and advice about what to do if you're scared about something.

Remember, it is okay to feel afraid.

Now you can try to understand and face your fears!

Activities

These activities can help you to think more about how to manage feeling scared or afraid.

- Draw a before and after picture of yourself. Draw a picture of yourself looking afraid, before you did something scary. Then draw a picture of yourself looking happy after you did something you were afraid of doing. Give your pictures speech bubbles. What would your scared self say? What would your brave self say?

- Write or draw what you're afraid of and then tear it up into little pieces and put it in the bin, as if you're tearing up and throwing away your fear.

- Ask other people — friends and family — what scares them or used to scare them. What did they do about it? Draw a picture or write a story about it.

- Act out a scene of you facing up to your fear with a friend or someone in your family.

- Ollie and Sanjiv are camping in their tent in the garden, but they keep seeing scary shadows and hearing spooky sounds. Write them a letter telling them what you think they could do to help them not to feel scared.

- Monsters don't have to be scary! If you're afraid of monsters, draw a picture of one looking likeable, friendly or funny. Maybe your monster has a big smile or is wearing striped underwear or a silly hat.

- Even superheroes get scared, but they use their courage and are brave. Do you have a favourite superhero? What would a superhero do about the thing you're scared of? Write a story or draw a picture of a superhero doing something brave.

Notes for teachers, parents and carers

Children are scared when situations beyond their control, or situations they don't understand, shake their sense of safety. They get scared and afraid that something might hurt or harm them.

You can help your child by taking their fears seriously and encouraging them to talk about their feelings. Have empathy and relate to their feelings — in this case, fear and anxiety — rather than focusing on what your child is scared of. Don't dismiss your child's fears, telling them it's never going to happen or implying they're being silly. Recognise that the fear feels real to your child and it's causing him or her to feel anxious and afraid.

While acknowledging your child's fears, try to keep things light; don't make a big deal or fuss about your child's fear in front of them or other people. This will only serve to lower their self-esteem and make your child believe that it is wrong to be scared and they may stop sharing their fears with you. Tell your child that it's okay to share their fear and to ask for help.

Children need effective techniques and strategies to help them take control and feel in control. *Face Your Fears* explains ways in which your child can manage their fears. There's a range of strategies which you can help them with: making a plan to deal with what's frightening them, ideas for how to face fears one step at a time, and explaining how and why some scary things happen.

Although your child can read this book by themselves it will be more helpful for both of you if you could read it together. You might have some stories from your own childhood about something that you were scared of that you could share with them. What used to frighten you and what did you find comforting at those times?

Your child might want to read the book in one go. Others will find it easier to manage and understand to read a few pages at a time. Either way, there are lots of talking points. Ask your child questions such as: Have you ever tried that? What do you think of that idea? How could that work for you? Talk about the characters in the illustrations.

Having read the book and helped your child identify some strategies that could work for them, give them the opportunity to manage their fears at their own pace and with your support. With time, patience, support and encouragement from you, your child can learn to cope with and overcome their fears.

If, though, their fears are frequently causing them distress and leading them to avoid everyday situations and miss out, then it's worth seeking more advice, so do approach your doctor and ask for help. You can also get advice from youngminds.org.uk. Call their Parents Helpline on 0808 802 5544.